Joseph J Mickley

Brief account of murders by the Indians and the cause thereof in Northampton county, Penn'a

October 8th, 1763

Joseph J Mickley

Brief account of murders by the Indians and the cause thereof in Northampton county, Penn'a
October 8th, 1763

ISBN/EAN: 9783742846594

Manufactured in Europe, USA, Canada, Australia, Japa

Cover: Foto ©Thomas Meinert / pixelio.de

Manufactured and distributed by brebook publishing software
(www.brebook.com)

Joseph J Mickley

Brief account of murders by the Indians and the cause thereof in Northampton county, Penn'a

BRIEF ACCOUNT

OF

MURDERS BY THE INDIANS,

AND

THE CAUSE THEREOF,

IN

NORTHAMPTON COUNTY, PENN'A.,

October 8th, 1763.

BY JOS. J. MICKLEY.

PHILADELPHIA:

THOMAS WILLIAM STUCKEY, PRINTER,
57 NORTH SEVENTH STREET.

1875

STUCKEY., PRINTER, 67 NORTH SEVENTH STREET.

TO THE MEMORY OF

John Jacob Mickley and his Descendants

THESE PAGES ARE

RESPECTFULLY DEDICATED BY HIS GREAT GRANDSON

The Author.

PREFACE.

GREEABLY to invitation, a large number of the descendants of JOHN JACOB MICKLEY (the first of that name in America) assembled on the farm, formerly his property, in North Whitehall Township, Lehigh County, where the Indians murdered two of his children, and also the family of John Schneider, on the adjoining farm, the 8th of October, 1763. In commemoration of that event, the following paper was prepared and read, October 8th, 1863. At that time I had no intention of publishing the same, but having been repeatedly urged by some of my relations and several esteemed friends, finally concluded to have it printed: it may, however, be of little or no interest, except perhaps to some of the numerous descendants of our ancestor JOHN JACOB MICKLEY.

In connection with this, it may not be out of place, and acceptable to some, to give such information of our

ancestors as has been handed down to us, partly from
documents, and partly by tradition. Traditional accounts,
however, though generally based on some truths, become,
in course of time, very much distorted and augmented, so
that not much reliance can be placed on them unless sup-
ported by documentary evidence; therefore some part of
my statement about our ancestors may require correction.
Bancroft says, very justly: "Memory is an easy dupe, and
tradition a careless story-teller."

From what I have been able to gather, it appears that
our family is descended from French Huguenots, the name
having originally been written MICHELET, but corrupted,
and variously written MIQUELET, MÜCKLI, &c., and finally
anglicized into the present form, MICKLEY: that during
the persecution of the Huguenots in France, they emigrated to the bordering Dukedom of Deux Ponts (Zwei-
brücken), then a part of the German Empire; where they
were unmolested in the exercise of their religion.

I have not been able to ascertain whether our ancestor
JOHN JACOB, or any other of them, was born in Deux
Ponts. When, during my visit there in the year 1869,
the records were examined at my request, I felt very
much disappointed in being told that nothing could be
found to show that such a family had ever resided in that
country; and, if it ever existed there, it must have been
recorded in that office, but that record is now lost.

It may not be surprising that the records are missing, after the enactment of such stringent laws against the Huguenots during the reign of the French King Louis XIV. For instance: the edict of 1681, which deprived them of nearly all their civil rights; the imperious order given to burn all their books; and the revocation of the Edicts of Nantes, October 22d, 1685. In the burning of their churches and books, probably all their church records shared the same fate with the general destruction, excepting such as may have been carried out of the country by the refugees. To this may be added that, through the devastation of the Palatinate and other German provinces by the French in the reign of the same King Louis XIV., many valuable documents were irretrievably lost.

We have, however, authentic information that our ancestor JOHN JACOB MICKLEY was born in Europe, in the year 1697, that he came to America in the ship Hope, of London, from Amsterdam, Holland, arriving in Philadelphia August 28th, 1733. He was married in this country to ELIZABETH BARBARA, daughter of ULRICH BURKHALTER, and settled in Whitehall Township, Northampton County, now North Whitehall, Lehigh County, and died in August, 1769. He left three sons and two daughters, viz. :—

JOHN JACOB, the eldest, my grandfather, who settled on a tract of land bordering on the village of Hockendauqua, in South Whitehall, Lehigh County: he had six sons and

four daughters. A number of his descendants still reside in that county.

JOHN MARTIN, the other son, sold the old homestead, and moved to and settled in Adams County, near Gettysburg, in the year 1794. He had four sons and five daughters. Many of his descendants are living in different parts of that county.

JOHN PETER, the third and youngest son, of whose escape from the Indians an account is given on the following pages, was in the military service against the Indians, and in the war of the Revolution, during the whole time of its continuance, in the capacity of fifer. He was in the battle of Germantown. At the close of the war he married, and settled in Bedminster Township, Bucks County, about the year 1784. He had two sons and eight daughters. Some of his descendants are still living in Bucks County, and one daughter, Mrs. STATZELL, eighty-eight years of age (yet very active), besides other descendants, are living in Philadelphia.

One daughter of JOHN JACOB MICKLEY, the first, became the wife of ANDREW MILLER, who resided in Linn Township, Lehigh County. She had no children.

The other daughter was married to PETER DESHLER, of Whitehall Township. By him she had three sons and one daughter. After the death of DESHLER, she married MICHAEL BIEBER, of Allen Township, in Northampton County. She had no children by BIEBER.

In preparing this account about the Indians, I have drawn from the most reliable authorities, and rejected many incredible verbal stories about Indian affairs which had been added in course of time, so that the statements may be tolerably correct. I cannot omit to express my great satisfaction in having visited JOHN PETER MICKLEY, in Bucks, and his sister, Mrs. BIEBER, in Northampton County, in the year 1819, and obtained many facts from them in relation to this matter: whatever the one related to me, was corroborated by the other. From them I also learned that the 8th of October, 1763, was one of those clear, pleasant days which have frequently been experienced at that time of the year. Owing to the occurrence of the Indian murders, that day has always been mentioned by our family as the beginning of Indian Summer.

In case anything has been misrepresented on these pages, I can only say that it was unintentional, and thus commend it to the judgment of the reader with my compliments.

JOSEPH J. MICKLEY.

PHILADELPHIA, *October 8th*, 1875.

BRIEF ACCOUNT

OF

Murders by the Indians, and the Cause thereof,

IN NORTHAMPTON COUNTY, PA.

WE have assembled here to-day, October 8th, 1863, to commemorate the Centennial Anniversary of the murders committed by the Indians in this and other parts of old Northampton County. I shall endeavor to show the cause of the irritation of the Indians, and then relate the events of the 8th of October, 1763, which not only created great consternation and cast gloom on the inhabitants of this part of the country, but also alarmed the Government of the Province of Pennsylvania.

Any outrage committed on the inhabitants of a community ought to excite an interest in every member of that community to inquire into and investigate the cause of such outrage. I presume that, after the lapse of one hundred years, an impartial statement can be made about

11

the origin of those murders without risk of giving offence
to any one; as, during or immediately after such an event,
the injured parties are generally more or less excited and
prejudiced, it is difficult to arrive at the facts, and, when
obtained, even hazardous to relate them until the excite-
ment is over. It is evident, from the following statements, that the Indians had sufficient cause to be exasperated through the bad acts of some of the white people.

"In the summer of the year 1763, some friendly Indians from a distant place came to Bethlehem to dispose of
their peltry for manufactured goods and necessary imple-
ments of husbandry. Returning home well satisfied, they
put up the first night at a tavern,[1] eight miles distant from
Bethlehem. The landlord not being at home, his wife
took the liberty of encouraging the people who frequented
her house for the sake of drinking, to abuse those Indians, adding, 'that she would freely give a gallon of rum
to any one of them that would kill one of these black
devils.' Other white people from the neighborhood came
in during the night, who also drank freely, made a great
deal of noise, and increased the fears of those poor Indians, who,—for the greatest part understood English,—
could not but suspect something bad was intended against
their persons. They were, however, not otherwise dis-
turbed; but in the morning, when after a restless night

---

[1] John Stenton's tavern.

they were preparing to set off, they found themselves robbed of some of the most valuable articles they had purchased, and on mentioning this to a man who appeared to be the bar-keeper, they were ordered to leave the house. Not being willing to lose so much property, they retired to some distance into the woods, when, some of them remaining with what was left them, the others returned to Bethlehem and lodged their complaint with a justice of the peace. The magistrate gave them a letter to the landlord, pressing him without delay to restore to the Indians the goods that had been taken from them. But, behold! when they delivered that letter to the people of the inn, they were told in answer, that if they set any value on their lives they must make off with themselves immediately. They well understood that they had no other alternative, and prudently departed without having received back any of their goods. Arrived at Nescopeck, on the Susquehanna, they fell in with some other Delaware Indians, who had been treated much in the same manner, one of them having his rifle stolen from him. Here the two parties agreed to take revenge in their own way for those insults and robberies for which they could obtain no redress, and this they determined to do as soon as war should be again declared by their nation against the English."—*Heckewelder's Account of the Indian Nations, page 332.*[1]

---

[1] *Note by Heckewelder.*—"This relation is authentic. I have received it from the mouth of the chief of the injured party, and

Scarcely had these Indians left, when, in another place,
about fourteen miles distant from Stenton's, another outrage was committed, of which the following account is
given in Loskiel's History of the Missions of the Indians
in America:—

"In August, 1763, Zachary and his wife, who had left
the congregation in Wechquetank[1] (where they had belonged, but left some time previous), came on a visit, and
did all in their power to disquiet the minds of the brethren respecting the intentions of the white people. A
woman called Zippora was persuaded to follow them. On
their return they staid at the Buchkabuchka[2] over night,
where Captain Wetterholt lay with a company of soldiers,
and went unconcerned to sleep in a hay-loft. But in the

his statement was confirmed by communications made at the time
by two respectable magistrates of the county. Justice Geiger's
letter to Tim. Horsfield proves this fact."

The Rev. John Heckewelder was born in Bedford, England,
March 12th, 1743. He came to America, with his parents, when
quite young: during forty years was a missionary among the Indians in different parts of this country, exposed to many hard-
ships and perils. He wrote several works on the Indians, which
are instructive and interesting on account of his having been fa-
miliar with their language, manners, and customs. He died at
Bethlehem, January 21st, 1823.

[1] Weckquetank was on Poca-poca (Head's) Creek, north of the
Blue Mountain; settled by Moravian Indians.

[2] Buchkabuchka. Heckewelder gives the following explanation
to this word:—"This is the name the Munseys have for the Lehigh Water Gap. The word implies:—'Mountains butting oppo-
site each other.'" At this place the Lehigh River runs through
the Blue Mountain.

night they were surprised by the soldiers. Zippora was thrown down upon the threshing-floor and killed; Zachary escaped out of the house, but was pursued, and with his wife and little child put to the sword, although the. mother begged for their lives upon her knees."

To these outrageous acts the conduct of Jonathan Dodge, a lieutenant in Captain Nicholaus Wetterholt's company,[1] added greatly to exasperate the Indians. This person,

---

[1] Johann Nicholaus Wetterholt arrived in Philadelphia, October 22d, 1754, in the ship Halifax, Thomas Coatam, captain, from Rotterdam. He was either a Hollander or a German,—most likely the latter. In the same ship came a large number of German emigrants. He entered the military service, probably soon after his arrival in this country, as it appears by his having been commissioned Captain in the First Battalion Pennsylvania Regiment, December 21st, 1755, and by the different sums of money paid to him for his and his company's services, and for provisions, viz.:—

1756.—April 29.—To Captain John Nicholaus Wetterholt, for his Company's pay,.		£332 3s. 0d.
" May 28.—To Captain John Nicholaus Wetterholt, for pay for himself and Company, and allowance for thirty-six guns furnished by his men, .		166 5s. 0d.
" June 21.—Samuel Depuy, in full, for his account, for purchasing provisions for a detachment of Captain Wetterholt's Company,		33 1s. 8d.
" Dec'r 15.—Samuel Depuy's order for victualling Captain Wetterholt's Company, &c.,		108 1s. 8d.

In the year 1762, Captain Nicholaus Wetterholt resided in Heidelberg Township, Northampton County, now Lehigh, and his name is on the tax list of 1764, at the same place.

who had been sent by Richard Hockley, of Philadelphia, with a letter to Timothy Horsfield,[1] dated July 14th, 1763, recommending him as "very necessary for the service," proved to be very troublesome soon after he entered the same. He committed many atrocious acts against his fellow-soldiers and the inhabitants of Northampton County, and particularly the Indians, which is proved by witnesses and his own statements, viz.:—

In a letter to Timothy Horsfield, dated August 4th, 1763, Dodge writes: "Yesterday there were four Indians came to Ensign Kern's. . . . I took four rifles and fourteen deer-skins from them, weighed them, and there was thirty-one pounds." After the Indians had left him, he continues:—"I took twenty men, and pursued them, . . . then I ordered my men to fire, upon which I fired a volley on them, . . . could find none dead or alive."

These happened to be friendly Indians, who had come

---

[1] Timothy Horsfield was born in Liverpool, England, in April, 1708. He emigrated to America, and settled on Long Island, in 1725; moved to Bethlehem in 1749; was appointed Justice of the Peace for Northampton County in May, 1752; commissioned Lieutenant and Colonel, and as such had the superintendence and direction of the two military companies commanded by the two Captains Wetterholt, which were ranging along the frontier; they sent their reports to him, and he corresponded with the Government at Philadelphia. Mr. Horsfield was of great service to the Government, as well as to the frontier inhabitants. He resigned both offices in December, 1763, and died at Bethlehem, March 9th, 1773.

from Shamokin, on their way to Bethlehem. Jacob Warner, a soldier in Nicholaus Wetterholt's company, made the following statement, September 9th:—That he and Dodge were searching for a lost gun, when, about two miles above Fort Allen, they saw three Indians painted black. Dodge fired upon them, and killed one; Warner also fired upon them, and thinks he wounded another; but two escaped: the Indians had not fired at them. The Indian was scalped; and, on the 24th, Dodge sent Warner with the scalp to a person in Philadelphia, who gave him eight dollars for it. These were also friendly Indians.

On the 4th of October, Dodge was charged with disabling Peter Frantz, a soldier; for striking him with a gun, and ordering his men to lay down their arms if the Captain should blame him about the scalp. In a letter of this date, Captain N. Wetterholt wrote to Timothy Horsfield: "If he (Dodge) is to remain in the company, not one man will remain. I never had so much trouble and uneasiness as I have had these few weeks; and if he continues in the service any longer, I don't purpose to stay any longer. I intend to confine him only for this crime."

On the 5th of October, Captain Nicholaus Wetterholt put Lieutenant Jonathan Dodge under arrest "for striking and abusing Peter Frantz," and sent him in charge of Captain Jacob Wetterholt, Sergeant Lawrence McGuire, and some soldiers, to Timothy Horsfield, at Bethlehem. On the 6th of October, Dodge was taken before Timothy Horsfield. I have no information of what took place there, but he was

2

no doubt examined, reprimanded, and released from arrest,
for he was with Captain Jacob Wetterholt[1] and party on
the 7th, at the house of John Stenton, on their return to
Fort Allen. At that time a great many of the Indians
were peaceably and friendly disposed toward the whites,
particularly those who had adopted a civilized life under
the instructions of the Moravian missionaries: it was
therefore necessary that the officers and others should
have been particularly cautious in their dealings and
intercourse with them, as the war feeling was then strong

[1] Johann Jacob Wetterholt came to this country in the same
vessel with his brother Nicholaus. He was commissioned Lieutenant in Major Parson's Town Guard, December 21st, 1755; in
April 19th, 1756, as Lieutenant, stationed at Dietz's; and as Captain,
in September 21st, of the same year; 1757, September 2d, he was
paid, for enlisting 53 men in the Provincial service, £88 6s. 6d.
Captain Jacob Wetterholt possessed undaunted courage, which
was accounted for in his firmly believing he had the power of
making himself invulnerable (kugelfest); that is, that he could
not be killed by a gun shot; he was therefore well suited for the
military service on the frontier. He knew very well that the
Indians intended to revenge themselves on the white people for
injuries received from some of the soldiers and others, and were
watching an opportunity to come upon them by surprise: he
eluded their vigilance, however, until that fatal morning of October 8th, 1763, when the house of John Stenton was attacked, where
he and Sergeant Lawrence McGuire were mortally wounded, and
afterward conveyed to Bethlehem by Lieutenant Jonathan Dodge,
who was paid on October 11th, "for bringing the wounded to Bethlehem, 9s. 9d., and for horse-keeping, 7s. 9d.,—17s. 6d." Captain
Wetterholt died on the following morning at the Crown Inn,
and was buried in the graveyard adjacent. In 1762, he resided in
Linn Township, now Lehigh County; his widow still resided
there in 1764, as per tax list. George Wetterholt, formerly sheriff
of Lehigh County, living in Allentown, is his grandson.

against the whites, so that the least provocation would
excite them to hostilities. It may have been difficult to
discriminate between the friendly and hostile Indians, but
the true policy would have been, to treat all in such a manner as to dispose them to peace. Unfortunately, a serious
cause of complaint of the Indians then was, that the white
people would too often act dishonestly in their dealings
and intercourse with them. When, in addition to this
pernicious practice,—which still exists to a considerable
extent,—officers and others having influence or power,
and whose duty it is to establish peaceable relations with
the Indians, set a bad example by abusing, robbing, and
murdering them, for which they have no prospect of ob-
taining redress, it is not at all surprising that the injured
party should become exasperated, and be determined on
taking revenge on the first opportunity.

On the 7th of October, Captain Jacob Wetterholt, with
his party, left Bethlehem, on their way to Fort Allen;
arrived at and lodged the following night at the house
of John Stenton, who kept a store and tavern, situated in
the Irish settlement, about a mile north of Howertown,
in Allen Township, Northampton County. Against this
house the Indians burned with revenge, on account of
injuries received there: they may also have had information that Lieutenant Dodge, an object of their hatred,
was with the Wetterholt party, and thought there would
now be an opportunity to take revenge on him as well
as on the Stentons. However that may have been, Cap-

tain Wetterholt must certainly have known that the Indians were highly exasperated against that house; it is, therefore, unaccountable why he did not have a guard stationed outside of it (which it appears was not done), as the greatest vigilance was required against a surprise by them. The Indians approached the house, unperceived and undiscovered, during the night; and when the door was opened before day, on the morning of the memorable 8th of October, by the servant of Captain Wetterholt, he was shot at and instantly killed. Captain Wetterholt and Sergeant McGuire were also shot at and dangerously wounded. John Stenton was shot dead.

The wounded were taken to Bethlehem, where Captain Wetterholt died the next day.

The redoubtable Lieutenant Dodge felt himself in a critical situation, as is evinced by his letter to Timothy Horsfield, here given verbatim:—

"John Stenton's, Oct. the 8, 1763.

"Mr. Hosfield, Sir, Pray send me help for all my men are killed But one, and Captn. Wetterholt js amost Dead, he is shot through the Body, for god sake send me help.

These from me to serve my contry and king so long as j live

Send me help or I am a Dead man

this from me Ljⁿt Dodge

sarg! meguire is shot through the body ——

Pray send up the Doctor for god sake."

Timothy Horsfield sent an express to Daniel Hunsicker, Lieutenant in Captain Jacob Wetterholt's company, with the following letter, to inform him of this disaster:—

BETHLEHEM, Oct. 8, 1763.

"SIR:—This morning, at about break of day, a number of Indians attacked the inhabitants of Allen's Town (Allen Township); have killed several, and wounded many more. Your Captain, who was here yesterday, lays at the house of John Stenton, at Allen's Town, wounded. Several of the soldiers have been killed. I send to Simon Heller, and request him to send a safe hand with it, that you may receive it as quick as possible. Now is the time for you and the men to exert yourselves in defence of the frontier, which I doubt not you will do. I expect to hear from you when you have any news of importance. Send one of your worst men: as it will be dangerous in the day time, send him in the night. The enclosed letter to Mr. Grube[1] I desire you send as soon as possible.

I am, &c., TIMOTHY HORSFIELD.

To LIEUTENANT HUNSICKER, *Lower Smithfield.*"

A detailed account of the different murders was sent by T. Horsfield, with a messenger,[2] to the Governor, at Philadelphia. It was published in the *Pennsylvania Gazette* of October 13th, 1763, printed by Benjamin Franklin, of which a copy is here annexed:—

---

[1] The Rev. B. D. Grube was a Moravian Missionary at Wechquetank.

[2] John Bacher, who was paid for this service, Oct. 12, £2 10s. 4d.

"On Sunday night last an express arrived from Northampton County, with the following melancholy account, viz. :—That on Saturday morning, the 8th inst., the house of John Stenton, about eight miles from Bethlehem, was attacked by Indians, as follows : Captain Wetterholt, with a party belonging to Fort Allen, being at that house, and intending to set out early for the fort, ordered a servant to get his horse ready, who was immediately shot down by the enemy; upon which the Captain, going to the door, was also fired at, and mortally wounded; that then a sergeant attempted to pull in the Captain and to shut the door, but he was likewise dangerously wounded; that the Lieutenant next advanced, when an Indian jumped upon the bodies of the two others and presented a pistol to his breast, which he put a little aside, and it went off over his shoulder, whereby he got the Indian out of the house and shut the door; that the Indians after this went round to a window, and as Stenton was getting out of bed shot him, but not dead, and he breaking out of the house ran about a mile, when he dropped and died; that his wife and two children ran down into the cellar, where they were shot at three times, but escaped; that Captain Wetterholt, finding himself growing very weak, crawled to a window, and shot an Indian dead, it was thought, as he was in the act of setting fire to the house with a match, and that upon this the other Indians carried him away with them, and went off. Captain Wetterholt died soon after." [1]

---

[1] A similar account also appeared in the *Philadelphische Staatsbote,*

Extract of a letter from Bethlehem, October 9th, from the same paper:—

"Early this morning came Nicholas Marks, of White-hall Township, and brought the following account, viz. : That yesterday, just after dinner, as he opened his door, he saw an Indian standing about two poles from the house, who endeavored to shoot at him; but, Marks shutting the door immediately, the fellow slipped into a cellar, close to the house. After this, said Marks went out of the house, with his wife and an apprentice boy,[1] in order to make their escape, and saw another Indian standing behind a tree, who tried also to shoot at them, but his gun missed fire. They then saw the third Indian running through the orchard; upon which they made the best of their way, about two miles off, to Adam Deshler's place, where twenty men in arms were assembled, who went first to the house of JOHN JACOB MICKLEY, where they found a boy and a girl lying dead, and the girl scalped. From thence they went to Hans Schneider's and said

printed by Heinrich Miller, in the German language, of October 17th, 1763.

[1] This apprentice boy was the late George Graff, of Allentown, then fifteen years of age. He ran to Philip Jacob Schreiber (my maternal grandfather) with the news of these murders. He was Captain of a company in the Revolutionary war. In 1786, he resigned as Collector of the Excise, and was Sheriff of Northampton County in the years 1787, '88, and '89. For three years he was a member of the Legislature, then holding its sessions in Philadelphia, from December 3d, 1793, to December, 1796. He lived many years in Allentown, where he died in 1835, in the 88th year of his age.

Marks' plantations, and found both houses on fire, and a
horse tied to the bushes.　They also found said Schneider,
his wife and three children, dead in the field, the man and
woman scalped; and, on going farther, they found two
others wounded, one of whom was scalped.　After this,
they returned with the two wounded girls to Adam Deshler's,[1] and saw a woman, Jacob Alleman's wife, with a

---

[1] Adam Deshler lived on the north bank of the Coplay* (Kolapechka) Creek, in the stone house built by him in the year 1760,
which is yet in a good state of preservation, and inhabited.　Adjoining this house on the north was a large frame building, suffi-
ciently large for quartering twenty soldiers, and for military stores.
This place was, during the Indian troubles, a kind of military post.
I remember well having seen that frame building, partly in ruins,
about sixty years ago.　Mr. Deshler was employed to furnish
provisions for the Provincial forces, as seen in his account with
the province of Pennsylvania (vide Votes of the Assembly):—

1756.—Feb. 26.—To Adam Deshler, for provisions furnished to Captain Wetterholt's Company,		£59 18s. 11¼d.
1756.—May 28.—To Adam Deshler, for provisions furnished to Captain Wetterholt's Company,		47 11s. 2d.
"　Oct. 29.—To Adam Deshler, for provisions furnished to Captain Wetterholt's Company, and the Provincial forces,		259 18s. 7d.
1757.—Apr. 16.—To Balliet and Deshler, for provisions supplied the forces at Forts Allen, Norris, and Hamilton,		807 4s. 11¼.
"　Aug. 26.—To Deshler and Balliet, for provisions supplied Provincial forces and Indians,		996 9s. 11d.

* Coplay is a corruption from Kolapechka, which was the name of an Indian, the
son of the Shawano Indian Chief Paxanosa. He lived at the head of the creek
named after him, on friendly terms with the white inhabitants. He was an honest
and trustworthy man. Timothy Horsfield employed him on several occasions to
carry messages to the Governor at Philadelphia.

child, lying dead in the road, and scalped. The number of Indians, they think, was about fifteen or twenty. I cannot describe the deplorable condition this poor country is in: most of the inhabitants of Allen's Town and other places are fled from their habitations. Many are in Bethlehem, and other places of the Brethren, and others farther down the country. I cannot ascertain the number killed, but think it exceeds twenty. The people of Nazareth, and other places belonging to the Brethren, have put themselves in the best posture of defence they can; they keep a strong watch every night, and hope, by the blessing of God, if they are attacked, to make a good stand."

"In a letter from the same county, of the 10th instant, the number killed is said to be twenty-three, besides a great many dangerously wounded: that the inhabitants are in the utmost distress and confusion, flying from their places, some of them with hardly sufficient to cover themselves, and that it was to be feared there were many houses, &c., burned, and lives lost that were not then known. And by a gentleman from the same quarter we are informed, that it was reported, when he came away, that Yost's mill, about eleven miles from Bethlehem, was de-

---

" Nov. 8.—To Deshler and Balliet, for provisions supplied Provincial forces and Indians, ... 550 19s. 5d.

1758.—June 9.—To Levan and Deshler, for provisions delivered sundry Companies, . 1354 4s. 4d.

stroyed, and all the people that belonged to it, excepting a young man, cut off."

After the deplorable disaster at Stenton's house, the Indians plundered James Allen's house, a short distance off; after which they attacked Andrew Hazlet's house, half a mile from Allen's, where they shot and scalped a man. Hazlet attempted to fire on the Indians, but missed, and he was shot himself, which his wife, some distance off, saw. She ran off with two children, but was pursued and overtaken by the Indians, who caught and tomahawked her and the children in a dreadful manner; yet she and one of the children lived until four days after, and the other child recovered. Hazlet's house was plundered. About a quarter of a mile from there, the Indians burned down Kratzer's house, probably after having plundered it. Then a party of Indians proceeded to a place on the Lehigh, a short distance above Siegfried's Bridge, to this day known as the "Indian Fall" or Rapids, where twelve Indians were seen wading across the river by Ulrich Schowalter, who then lived on the place now owned by Peter Troxel. Schowalter was at that time working on the roof of a building, the site of which being considerably elevated above the river Lehigh, he had a good opportunity to see and count the Indians, who, after having crossed the river, landed near Leisenring's mountain. It is to be observed, that the greater part of this township was at that time still covered with dense forests, so that the

Indians could go from one place to another almost in a straight line, through the woods, without being seen. It is not known that they were seen by any one but Scho-walter, until they reached the farm of JOHN JACOB MICK-LEY (my great-grandfather), where they encountered three of his children, two boys and a girl, in a field under a chestnut tree gathering chestnuts. The children's ages were:—Peter, eleven; Henry, nine; and Barbary, seven; who, on seeing the Indians, began to run away. The little girl was overtaken not far from the tree by an Indian, who knocked her down with a tomahawk. Henry had reached the fence, and, while in the act of climbing it, an Indian threw a tomahawk at his back, which, it is supposed, instantly killed him. Both of these children were scalped. The little girl, in an insensible state, lived until the fol-lowing morning. Peter, having reached the woods, hid himself between two large trees which were standing near together, and, surrounded by brushwood, he remained quietly concealed there, not daring to move for fear of being discovered, until he was sure that the Indians had left. He was, however, not long confined there; for, when he heard the screams of the Schneider family, he knew that the Indians were at that place, and that his way was clear. He escaped unhurt, and ran with all his might, by way of Adam Deshler's, to his brother, JOHN JACOB MICKLEY (my grandfather), to whom he communicated the melan-cholly intelligence. From this time Peter lived a number of years with his brother JOHN JACOB, after which he

settled in Bucks County, where he died in the year 1827,
at the age of seventy-five. One of his daughters, widow
of the late Henry Statzel (who I am pleased to see here),
informed me, among other matters, of a remarkable fact
related by her father, namely : that the MICKLEY family
owned at that time a very large and ferocious dog, which
had a particular antipathy to Indians ; and it was believed
by the family, that it was owing to the dog the Indians
did not make an attack on their house, and thus the
destruction of their lives was prevented. JOHN JACOB
MICKLEY and Ulrich Flickinger, then on their way to
Stenton's, being attracted by the screams of the Schneiders,
hastened to the place where, a short time before, was
peace and quietness, and saw the horribly mangled bodies
of the dead and wounded, and the houses of Marks and
Schneider in flames. The dead were buried on Schneider's farm.

It is well known that, when the Indians become exasperated through real or imaginary injuries, they consider
themselves bound to take revenge on their enemies, without regard to age or sex ; it therefore frequently happens
that the innocent suffer equally with the guilty.

It may perhaps be proper to state in this place, that
the MICKLEY family, as well as that of Schneider's, were
among those who suffered innocently, not a single instance
being known of their ever having been guilty of molesting

the Indians. Heckewelder says: "The Indians, after leaving this house (Stenton's), murdered by accident an innocent family, having mistaken the house [1] they meant to attack; after which they returned to their homes."— *Heckewelder's Account of the Indian Nations, page 334.*

The people in those parts were poorly prepared for defending themselves against any attacks by the Indians; even in Allentown, where a great number had gone for safety, and little aid could be expected, as appears by the following letters to Governor James Hamilton:—

Copy of a Letter by Joseph Roth, given verbatim.

"Formation of a Company in Northampton Co., 1763.

"NORTHAMPTON TOWN, *the 10th, this instant, October,* 1763.

"To the Honarable JAMES HAMBLETON, Esqr, Lieutennent Governeur and Commander in Chief of the Province of Pensylvania, New Cassel, Cent, and Sasox, on Delawar,

"We send Greeting:—As I, Joseph Roth, of Northampton Town, Church Minister, of the ninth of this instant, October, as I was preaching, the people came in such numbers that I was abliged to quit my sarmon; and the same time Cornel James Bord was in Town; and I, the aforesaid minister, spoke with Cornel Bord concerning this

---

[1] It was generally believed that the Indians mistook this house for that of Paulus Balliet's, which they intended to attack. Mr. Balliet lived at the place now Ballietsville, and kept a store and tavern, similar to that of John Stenton's.

afarres of the Indians, and we found the inhabitance that the had nither Gons, Powder nor Lead, to defend themselves, and that Cornel Bord had latly spoke with his Honour. He had informed him, that we would assist them with gons and ammunition, and he requested of me to write to your Honour, because he was just seting of for Lancester, and the inhabitance of the town had not chose their officers at the time he set off, so we, the inhabitance of the said town hath unahimus chose George Wolf, the bearer hereof, to be Captain, and Abraham Rinker to be Lieutennent; we hose names are under writen, promiss to obey to this mentioned Captain and Lieutennent, and so we hope his Honor will be so good and send us 50 gons, 100 pound of powder, and 400 pound lead, 150 stans for the gons. These from your humble servant, Remaining under the Protection of our Lord Jesus Christ.

"JOSEPH ROTH, *Minister*.

"The names of the Company of this said Northampton Town:—

"GEORGE WOLF, *Captain*,	DAVID DESCHLER,
ABRAHAM RINKER, *Lieutenant*,	JOHN MARTIN DŒRR,
PHILIP KUGLER,	PETER ROTH,
PETER MILLER,	FRANTZ KEFFER,
FREDERICK SCHÆKLER,	JACOB MOHR,
LEONHARD ABEL,	MARTIN FREHLICH,
TOBIAS DITTIS,	GEORGE LAUER,
LORENZ HOUCK,	DANIEL NUNNENMACHER,
SIMON BRENNER,	PETER SCHWAB,
JACOB WOLF,	ABRAHAM SÆVITZ,
SIMON LAGUNDACKER,	JOHN SCHNECK,
GEORGE NICHOLAUS,	JOHN GEORGE SCHNEPF,

MICHAEL ROTHROCK."

Extract from Colonel James Burd's Letter to Governor Hamilton:—

LANCASTER, *October 17th,* 1763.

"SIR:—I arrived here on Monday night, from Northampton. I need not trouble your Honor with a relation of the misfortune of that county, as Mr. Horsfield told me he would send you an express, and inform you fully of what had happened. I will only mention, that in the town of Northampton (where I was at the time), there were only four guns, three of which unfit for use, and the enemy within four miles of the place.

"Respectfully yours,

JAMES BURD."

That these affairs also alarmed the Government of the Province of Pennsylvania, is evident from the fact that, when Governor James Hamilton had received information of the murders in Northampton County, he took the matter immediately in hand, called the attention of the Assembly to the subject, and recommended to it, in the strongest terms, to devise means for the protection of the frontier inhabitants, in the following extract from his message to the Assembly, dated October 15th, 1763 :—

"I am sensible it is very unusual to enter upon business of weight at your first meeting, that being set apart for, or employed in preparing the house for the better reception and dispatch of it at some future time; yet I flatter myself you will readily dispense with a custom, by no

means essential, in favor of the measure I have to recommend to you, which is of as great importance as can come
under your consideration; no less, indeed, than the safety
and preservation of the country. You will be pleased
then to know, that, within a few days past, I have received
well-attested accounts of many barbarous and shocking
murders, and other depredations, having been committed
by Indians on the inhabitants of Northampton County;
in consequence whereof, great numbers of those who
escaped the rage of the enemy have already deserted,
and are daily deserting their habitations; so that, unless
some effectual aid be speedily granted them, to induce
them to stand their ground, it is difficult to say where
those desertions will stop, or to how small a distance from
the Capital our frontier may be reduced.

"The Provincial Commissioners and I have, in consequence of the resolve of the Assembly of the 6th of July
last, done everything in our power for the protection of
the Province, pursuant to the trust reposed in us; but as
our funds are entirely exhausted, and even a considerable
arrear become due to the soldiers, and others employed by
the Government, for their pay, which we have not in our
power to discharge, it seems impossible that the forces
now on foot can be longer kept together, without a supply
is speedily granted for that purpose.

"I, therefore, gentlemen, in the most earnest manner
recommend to your immediate consideration the distressed
state of our unfortunate inhabitants of the frontier, who

are continually exposed to the savage cruelty of a merci-
less enemy, and request that you will, in your present
session, grant such a supply as, with God's assistance,
may enable us not only to protect our own people, but to
take a severe revenge on our perfidious foes, by pursuing
them into their own country; for which purpose there
prevails at present a noble ardor among our frontier
people, which in my opinion ought by all means to be
cherished and improved. I have, gentlemen, only one
thing more to recommend and request of you, which is,
that in contriving the ways and means for raising the
supply to be granted, you will carefully avoid whatever
may occasion a disagreement of opinion between you and
me, by means whereof your good intentions may be frus-
trated and defeated, as has unfortunately happened on
more than one occasion before, and particularly in the last
session of the late Assembly."— *Votes of the Assembly*,
Vol. V., p. 281.

The Assembly acted promptly in furnishing the proper
means for defence, by passing a bill on the 22d of October,
1763, viz.: "That the sum of twenty-four thousand pounds
be granted to his majesty, for raising, paying, and vic-
tualling eight hundred men (officers included), to be employed in the most effectual manner for the defence of
this Province."—*Ibid*, p. 282.

The Assembly also acted immediately on the following

petition, presented by Nicholas Marks, praying for the relief of the daughters of John Schneider:—

"*1765, May 15th.*—A petition from Nicholas Marks, next friend and brother-in-law to Magdalene and Dorothy Schneider, daughters of John Schneider, of Whitehall Township, in the County of Northampton, deceased, being both minors, was presented to the House and read, setting · forth, that on the eighth of October, in the year one thousand seven hundred and sixty-three, the said John Schneider, his wife, and three children, were most cruelly murdered by the Indians, at their dwelling house in Whitehall Township aforesaid, one of the children being supposed to be taken captive, having ever since been missing and never heard of; and the aforesaid girls barbarously wounded, one scalped, and left for dead upon the spot by the said enemy, whereby the whole remaining part of the family hath been left utterly impoverished. That one of the aforesaid girls, namely, Magdalene, through the mercy of God, and skill of the surgeons who attended her, has happily recovered of her wounds; but the other, named Dorothy, is still in a languishing condition, and subject to fits, whereof she has frequent returns. That the accounts annexed to the petition have been brought by the surgeons against the said Magdalene and Dorothy, and amount, together, to forty-four pounds, three shillings and eight pence, which the estate of their deceased father (after just debts are discharged) is insufficient to pay; neither is it in the power of either of the said sufferers to

make any compensation to the surgeons. Wherefore the petitioner prays the House to take the premises into consideration, and give orders to the Provincial Treasurer to pay off the said accounts as a public debt, or take such other method to discharge the same, and relieve a distressed and helpless family, as the House shall think proper."—*Ibid*, p. 411.

"*May 16th.*—The House resumed the consideration of the petition of Nicholas Marks, in behalf of Magdalene and Dorothy Snyder, sisters-in-law to the petitioner, and after some debate thereon, ordered: That Mr. Samuel Foulke, from Bucks, and Mr. George Taylor, from Northampton, be a committee to take the opinion of some physician in town upon the reasonableness of the surgeons' accounts annexed to said petition, and report the same to the House."—*Ibid*, p. 413.

2025062

"*May 18th.*—The members appointed to take the opinion of some physician in town, on the accounts of certain surgeons, for the cure of Magdalene and Dorothy Schneider, wounded by the Indians, delivered the said account at the table, with a certificate under the hands of Doctor Thomas Cadwalader and Doctor Phineas Bond, that they had examined the same, and do not find any of the charges therein contained exorbitant or unreasonable. Whereupon certificates were drawn at the table to John Matthew Otto, the Estate of Jacob Rein, deceased, and to Frederick

Spiegel, amounting in the whole to £44 3s. 8d., which,
being signed by the Speaker, were delivered to Mr. Taylor,
of the County of Northampton."—*Ibid*, pp. 418, 419.

When the condition of this part of the country is considered, in which, one hundred years ago, a few families
were living, without protection, in a wilderness, deprived
of almost every comfort, exposed to attacks from wild
beasts and reptiles, and the danger of being murdered,
and have their property destroyed by hostile Indians, who
kept them constantly in such fear that the members of
the families bade each other farewell in the evening before
retiring, being under the impression that they might not
meet again on the next morning; when such a melancholy
state of affairs is compared with the present flourishing
condition, where now the people are living in peace, themselves and property protected, and where are seen numerous finely cultivated farms, with convenient habitations,
furnaces, manufactories, canals, railroads, improvements
in every branch of industry, and the comforts of a numerous population; when all this is considered, we are im-
pelled to profound gratitude. If any person exists who is
unable to appreciate these advantages and blessings, he
must be a heartless and ungrateful being, unworthy of
living in this community.

In the above I have presented such matter as I considered suitable on this occasion, and as might be agree-

able to, at least, some of the descendants of our forefather, JOHN JACOB MICKLEY. I shall be much pleased if, by the facts here presented, sufficient interest has been excited in any one (more capable than myself) to pursue the subject further, and produce a more complete history of the Indian troubles at that time in this part of the country. Fearing to have trespassed on your patience, and thanking you for your kind attention, I now conclude.

Stuckey, Printer, 57 North Seventh Street, Philadelphia.